Coffeehouse Meditations

In praise of *Coffeehouse Meditations* …

Nina Romano's *Coffeehouse Meditations* concentrates on odes and wry nods to Starbucks—American coffee with Italian roots—and surprisingly philosophical meditations about domestic life. Laundry, cooking, and driving are all jumping points for Romano's compassion and longing. Romano skillfully employs meditative prose blocks, tercets, and found text (such as Nabokov's journal and a neighbor's discarded diary) to extract and build the profound found in the ordinary.
—Denise Duhamel, *Ka-Ching! Two And Two, Queen for a Day*

Whether she is writing about sitting in a Starbucks or traveling the world, Nina Romano's poems breathe with intimacy, warmth, and a strong, vivid sense of place. While many writers spend time in coffeehouses, few of us actually write about being in them, particularly with Romano's wit and sharp powers of observation. Her travel poems are written with passion, zest, and a sense of wonder. They're not about the scenery—they're about the heart. Like *Cooking Lessons*, Romano's first book, *Coffeehouse Meditations* has a natural unity and clarity that should be the envy of any poet.
—Jim Daniels, *Revolt of the Crash-Test Dummies, Mr. Pleasant, In Line for the Exterminator*

Nina Romano's *Coffeehouse Meditations* brims chock-full with warm intelligence and delicate artistry. These charming poems cordially invite every reader—both stranger and friend—to "come in and be welcome." And what wonderful, companionable stories she tells! There's a great range of feeling in these poems—love and friendship, anger and frustration, as well as hunger in all its various manifestations. Through it all, Romano reminds us of the vividness of ordinary life, of "guitar music wafting toward me on a gentle summer breeze" and "butterfly bushes/almonding the very air…"
—Michael Hettich, *Many Loves, Flock and Shadow, Swimmer*

Dreams, Stationary Wind, Behind Our Memories, The Point of Touching

Nina Romano pays attention to the commonplace and celebrates our sacred days. Her elegiac and lyric voice gives praise to the seemingly mundane and sanctifies the ordinary. She knows how the terrible beauty in the world can seize us and save us—if we let it. Reading *Coffeehouse Meditations* is a joy and an exhilaration. This is work that matters.

    —John Dufresne, *Requiem, Mass., Love Warps the Mind a Little, Deep in the Shade of Paradise, Louisiana Power and Light*

Nina Romano is the principal poet of the School of Coffee House scribes. While the rest of us visit these nooks and simply ponder whether to foam or not, Romano digs deeper and finds a place and a prism through which to address what is vital: the rich nuances of marriage and family, the solace found in gardens, night skies, and faith. Samuel Coleridge, Auguste Rodin and other "gods of yore" make appearances, but what draws these poems together is that they are all mined from a curious and thoughtful heart.

    —Emma Trelles, *Little Spells,* poems and essays in *MiPOesias, Gulf Stream, New Millennium Writings,* the *Miami Herald, Newsday, Latina* magazine

Coffeehouse Meditations

Nina Romano

Kitsune Books

Quality books for eclectic readers

Coffeehouse Meditations

Kitsune Books
P.O. Box 1154
Crawfordville, FL 32326-1154

www.kitsunebooks.com
contact@kitsunebooks.com

Printed in USA
First printing in 2010

ISBN-13: 978-0-9819495-2-9
Library of Congress Control Number: 2009937522

Front cover art: Steve Stento, www.stevestento.com

Author portrait, back cover: Robert Hurth,
Tiffany Photographic Studio. www.tiffanyphoto.com

First Edition

For: My Link

Acknowledgements

For affording me the time to write, I offer my husband, Felipe Romano, a world of thanks.

I'd like to thank Anne C. Petty, editor of Kitsune Books, for reading the manuscript, and Leonard Nash for his friendship and faith in me as a poet and writer. I wish to express gratitude to Mona Birch, Marni Graff, Melissa Westemeier, and Denise Lanier for their attention to detail while reading and critiquing my poems.

To all those who read my poetry, or who listened to me read it, I'd like to extend a warm, heartfelt thank you: Jane Brownley, Rita Quinton, John Damon, Phil De Simone, Elaine Winer, Lauren Small, Marie Lovas, Mariana Damon, John Dufresne, and Emma Trelles.

And to those poets who have influenced my work on a personal level, I would like to convey sincere thanks: June Gould, Jim Daniels, Denise Duhamel, Campbell McGrath, Jesse Milner, Elisa Albo, Michael Hettich, Gregory Orr, C. K. Williams, Cathy Bowman, Li-Young Lee.

There are other poets, whom I would like to recognize for their wonderful work which has inspired my writing: Mary Oliver, Elizabeth Bishop, Walt Whitman, Dante Alighieri, Emily Dickinson, Edgar Allen Poe, Joy Harjo, Seamus Heaney, C.D. Wright, Louise Glück, Thomas Hardy, Samuel Coleridge, William Stafford, Peter Balakian.

Grateful acknowledgment is made to the editors of the following publications and online magazines, where these poems first appeared, some in different form:

A Little Poetry: "Butterfly Garden," "Between Itaka and Kefalonia," and "Sunday in New York"

By the Sea Times: "Beachcomber on His Break"

Driftwood: "Autumn Walk in Mizzling Rain," "Priest," and "Your Name"

Salt Lake City Weekly: "Apache Tears"

Rough-Writers INK: "Traveling," "Cottonwood Canyons"

Mangrove Review: "Pining," "Crucible of Yearning," and "Limerick"

Southern Women's Review: "Intricacies of Cicada Wings"

CONTENTS

I have set My rainbow in the clouds,
and it will be the sign of the covenant
between Me and the earth.

Genesis 9:13

Part I

Coffeehouse

CONCEPTUAL SUITE

On the car CD player she listens to Kate Bush's song about a widow,
watching her clothes in the dryer tangle and intertwine in a sexual
heap with her dead husband's. The erotic tryst of embraces in the words

of the widow—a window on a lost world, whoosh and swish with traffic
passing by. The driver struggles with the straw, slurping the dregs of the
Mocha Java Chip Frappuccino (whipped cream on top, bottom sludge)

a chip in the fat green straw blocks the ebb and flow of the delish drink
while she battles traffic on I-95 all the way home from her daughter's
in Jupiter. *I must be nuts*, she thinks. *Why don't I pull over? Why don't*

I take off the plastic top? Drink from the cup? Why didn't I order a simple
drink? Like a cold Cappuccino—but then realizes why. Starbucks stole
the coffeehouse idea from Italy's cafés—but screwed up one drink—

there's no such thing as cold cappuccino, because the kids behind
the machines think it needs froth. But that's just for hot which she didn't
want in the first place. Now in the rear view mirror a frantic cop waves

his hand, blaring lights and siren pulling her over, about to write a ticket,
for interfering with the traffic's ebb and flow, because she's crossed
into the HOV lane, so intent in sucking up that last chip. She thinks

to offer him a sip to placate his angry demeanor. If anyone needed
a Starbucks' coffee now, it's this FHP ogre with cropped hair walking
toward her, menacingly tapping his watch. Next time, she'll buy two—

just in case. A glance at the clock, unchanged since spring, she stashes
the cup beneath the seat, turns off the radio, smiles and says opening
the window, *Something wrong, officer? I wasn't speeding, was I?*

DEPICTION: UNWRITTEN WORDS ON THE WALL
AT STARBUCKS

The gods of yore proclaim
myths as yet unheard

and under a gray-mottled sky
flocks of goats graze,

a means of great riches
for the man by the lake's shore

and rivering out of him
come songs—soft as spring

willow speech compliant to fields,
shadowing and echoing over bends and bights,

to break like a porcelain bowl
heaved, smashed upon headland rocks;

he croons a lone tune,
crooking a long staff

to emphasize the words
as he punctures the earth

a refrain, a ballad of loneliness
staccato with spikes

spun in spirals slowly
from the unafraid man

as he hums a hymn
knowing the world

listens to the energies
that lie synergistically below

the Earth's surfaces
beneath the molten lava

or pyramids patiently awaiting …
yielding a prophet of changes.

HIS GESTURE

is so sweet,
I want to melt.

He's blond, a little taller than she
and stands behind her
as she orders Starbucks' cappuccino
rich and tall with froth on top.

He gently rubs her back,
his hand moves in tiny circles
that spiral up and down.
It is at once sensual,
yet tender and protective.

He loves her.
He nuzzles her back

then slowly lifts
and leans his head
onto her shoulder,
turning inward slightly

pushing back her hair
to kiss her bare neck,
and I want to swoon.
I want to be a part of this love
so private

yet made in such a public
display

so easily expressed.
Then I think of the times
when I was young
and my husband dropped

my hand in public.
So I will go home now
to caress the dog behind his ears
to feel his hot breath
on my cheek and on my neck.

AUTUMN IN DENVER

Sitting in the Denver Starbucks
on 16th Street, I spy a tiny
cricket on a pinecone
on the windowsill outside.

Yesterday I found the pinecone,
and not wanting to carry it around all day,
left it on this very spot, and now
I wish the windowpane were gone,

so I could reach out and say hello
to such a welcomed yet uninvited guest.
Uh-oh! He's hopped away from
safety on the sill to a dish.

He should've leapt to the autumn flowers.
If I shriek will someone trap him
with wiles and womanly ways?
Will a pioneer gun-totting gal of the old west

come round the corner to rescue him
at play among the blueberry muffin crumbs?
Oh dear, now here's a sweeper,
cleaning up and dusting that little critter

straight into a wastepaper pail
covering him up with a surplus
spiral bound University of Colorado
notebook. I watch as the sweeper

glides gingerly in between
the crowd holding coffee mugs.
He sets the little *creepus crawlus* free
in the softest patch of turf

near sweet-smelling yellow and rust
chrysanthemums, the same ones Mom's
bridesmaids carried on her wedding day—
seventy-two years ago, a thousand miles away.

WHAT'S DOING? OR HANGING AROUND STARBUCKS

Come in! Be welcome both stranger and friend, coffee drinkers, tea lovers, people watchers.

Come in and be welcome both stranger and friend, the girl who speaks Italian, the firemen and cops on breaks.

Come in and be welcome both stranger and friend, the wall that greets and the wall that speaks in tongues and gifted me poem # 2.

Come in and be welcome both stranger and friend, the green velvet chairs, so cushy and comfy, people at their ease, taking naps.

Come in and be welcome both stranger and friend, the lady who sits so straight typing on her laptop computer.

Come in and be welcome both stranger and friend, the man who writes so tiny you'd need a magnifying glass to read his Lilliputian notes.

Come in and be welcome both stranger and friend, the man in jeans and tee shirt with unkempt hair to his shoulders, who sits alone and stares.

Come in and be welcome both stranger and friend, the Starbucks worker reading sci-fi on recess, his hair silken blond one day, coal black the next.

Come in and be welcome both stranger and friend, Gloria Padilla Carlson, "I am Starbucks … mother of two, taste my *Dulce de Leche*."

SITTING IN STARBUCKS

A sleepless soul looks at pictures on the monitor
and wonders, Is anyone out there?

She shakes her head. Are you listening?
Dawn peeps in the sky as I watch her through the window

where she's alone except for her laptop,
the Starbucks' skeleton staff, and a tall paper cup

with logo that sits by a lit screen—
luminous, eerie halogen upon her face.

What's she thinking?
With keyboard and words

she expels, expunges, the exhausted night
with expectance of a silent, salient,

significant something ... a new day.
She wants to print out and scribble

I hate you! on his photo, now palimpsest
of echoed past; instead scrawls upon the screen:

I love you still! My heart aches a little,
it breaks for her, a crack that fissures,

splitting my heart into two:
one for her, one for me.

SAYOURDAY SATURDAY PROSE POEM IN SALUTE OF *DOPPIO ESPRESSO*

As I wait for my Jane to meet me for coffee, but she'll probably order a Chai tea, I think of *Waiting for Godot*. I am writing this on the Egyptian pink pad of paper that Jane gave me for Christmas with a Health Magazine subscription and a Fusion clear lip gloss that tastes delicious. I know because when my husband kisses me he asks for more. I'm sitting in Starbucks, the one we call the north campus—the one closest to her being the south campus—waiting for Jane to join me.

It's Saturday and my family is going out on tour on our Sea Ray, the *Makaira*, which means blue marlin in Latin, for the Air and Sea show—the last time I went I was a fantastic shade of chartreuse from rocking and bouncing in choppy waters. This may not be significant or earth-shattering, but this small freedom is great for me. I'll spend the day writing long, complicated sentences, trying for a Tolstoy effect in my Russian novel, past due to get into the eager mitts of my writing group, Screw Iowa!

Ah! There's Jane. I tell her that I've outgrown the single espresso, and for a long time drank a double loaded to the gills with luscious whirled and swirled, white frothy, yummy-to-the-tummy whipped cream, but ... then Lent came and I chided myself: forget and forgo, and penitently asked for just the double shots straight, no joyous loamy, lovely, frothy hillocks and mountainy peaks of cream like the top of Deer Valley in Park City to accompany it. But the forty Lenten days are passed, and the hum-drum life of simple double espresso came and went. Instead, there came a day, not long ago when somehow "triple" slipped from my tongue and I was penitent no more. No more the abject sinner in sackcloth and ashes! Now I'm a happy, coffee-guzzling addict in knee-ripped jeans and Starbucks tee, a dollop of whipped cream on the tip of my nose.

1-800-STARBUCKS
—For Cathy Bowman

As it happens, on May 19ᵗʰ, 2007, I received a postcard, & at first glance
it gleamed. On the left hand side haloed in a pure golden light two shot
glasses, frothy espresso pouring into them from a machine that might

be Italian like Faema, though I'm not sure. The other side of the card
is stark coffee brown with two printed words in white: THANK YOU.
My name & address are correct. Starbucks wants to thank me with

a gift of $5 to be loaded onto my card by May 17ᵗʰ. A glitch in dates?
Another glitch I find is the last four digits end in 1377. I look at all 7
of my cards stowed in various drawers & wallets, purses & pocket

books, the latest Lehane thriller. No such number! Now I'm thinking:
how then do the corporate heads know I'm spending all these green-
backs, do-re-mi & cashola on their frothy drinks?

I dial 1-800-Starbuc (no "ks") & speak to Dave. He's personable
& smart, offers to register my card, which I thought I'd already done.
He loads my card—the real one with my real numbers with five extra

shimoleons! to be spent at Starbucks … maybe? Ah, surely,
as I'm hooked on the espresso & the paper cups with wise & witty
sayings, only wish one of them were mine.

GROUNDS ... FREE

Coffee grounds for your garden, please help yourself,
the sign reads in a perky array of green fields and golden sun.

The sun and pastoral scene of the FREE ad
remind me of Otto's play land, our backyard

where free to roam, brave hunter dog, won't dunk his tootsies
in the pool even on the hottest south Floridian day.

His favorite pastime, cavorting in the garden—
he knows is his domain; he prances with squeak toy

or darts over the waylaid kayak, leaps midair
for a Wilson's yellow tennis ball,

quite deflated by his crushing canines.
He chases sassy squirrels, feisty opossums, gray doves,

transparent geckoes and emerald green iguanas diving off the dock,
but it's a guarantee if Otto ever got a sniff of Starbucks'

leftover coffee grounds sprinkled in my wooden planters
to aerate the basil's soil, or newly planted cilantro,

he'd most likely yelp like mad, an invitation to the new neighbor's dog
for a quick cup of bold java, hoping I'll lace it with Sambuca.

Or he'll twitch his nose, send fierce telegraphic barks across
the other fence for Mister Riley, the parti-colored pup next door.

And Riley's owner will pop over for a look-see
at the party, the equation now compounded ...

I'll have to serve the French fruit tarts set aside for tonight's dessert—
So as you can plainly see, and surely must agree,

I should insist you take down that sign, for nothing's free
about those grounds now, Starbucks, is there?

THE COFFEE POEM

Sitting in Starbucks across from Pompano Fashion Mall, waiting for my "hot date," AKA, my brother, I read the names on the shelves and my mind takes me to foreign lands. Who picks the coffee named *Casi Cielo*—almost heaven? Someone in Guatemala is a poet for sure, and this coffee, whose gold-crowned label reads, MEDIUM, is embellished with a romantic setting: a blond woman seated at a round white-clothed table, set with coffee carafe and cups, is being served by a swarthy open-shirted hunk! Who chooses the brand name: Columbia *Mariño Supremo* Medium from Latin America or Africa or Arabia as the package denotes? Does the picker know the coffee's name as he tugs the green beans from the branches? Does he know that the coffee will be roasted and bagged into burlap sacks to be transported in the holds of cargo ships that prison still the souls of brethren? Does he know that these bags will then be picked up by nets and dumped unceremoniously into trucks that will transport them to factories? And after the chucking and hauling, unloading, this cargo will be delivered to factories where the magic of bean selection will be employed. Does the picker know that then each bean will be hand selected and chosen as if a veiled bride to be handed up on the wedding altar of the conveyor belt to lead it further to be packaged into a rainbow-colored bag stamped with these exotic names? Does the picker know this parcel will be stacked up on a shelf with other bags equally as beautifully wrapped and even more mysteriously named than this one? Does the picker know that a sister awaits her brother in a Starbucks in Pompano Beach, Florida, at 4 pm on this first day of spring? Does the picker ever think of a woman sipping this bewitching brew, propelling mind-traveling thoughts of thanks to him for his toil in faraway fields, and cherishing this moment? *Mil gracias!*

GREETINGS TO THE GOURMAND OF GOURMET GROUND

Ah! To the gastronome.
Hurrah! To the connoisseur
Good day! Oh, thee epicure
Hark ye foodies!
Hail, drinkers of *café au lait*!

All aficionados, every last enthusiast
Beauteous buffs
Frank fanatics
Able, adept, accomplished admirers
Free-for-all, freaky fans

Adroit addicts of the Starbucks brew
It's to you, for you
And above all with you,
These words are penned!
O smart and savvy tasters

Of the elixir of life—
Served in a Starbucks logo paper cup
With wise, worldly witticisms
Imprinted upon them …
In future, who says mine won't be one?

DEAR ST. BUCKS

I abbreviated Starbucks
in an e-mail to a friend,
and came up with a new saint:
St. Bucks! Just what the Almighty needed.

Lordy, Lordy!
In a way it is a saint,
or at least a hallowed,
saintly place of refuge

having gotten me through
many a bleak day
when my writing was less
than brilliant ... like now.

My prayer: I come to thee,
oh blessed saint,
father, inventor, and elevator
of COFFEEHOUSES.

I supplicate upon my knees,
and place my needs before thee.
Oh, holy and devout,
worshiped and revered, dearest

Santo Bucks, kind and good saint,
intercede before the throne of heaven
on my behalf. I beg of you a favor:
please grant me one carbolic, coal tar,

catabolic, catastrophic,
considerably celebrated,
colossal coffee
to clear my head.

SEVEN HUNDRED PENNIES

In the coffeehouse of coffeehouses,
over cappuccino and croissant,
you tell me stories; one I love
about your grandparents.
He'd just come home from Iwo Jima,
thin, gaunt, taller than your grandma recalled,
and pale; she loved him as fiercely as before
he'd left, right after their three
month honeymoon. She was living
in Brooklyn then, and they packed
the old Studebaker her father lent her
and took off to see the States.

What a honeymoon that was! Oh yeah!
But there was a major glitch—
he couldn't pick up his government check
at the Air Force base in Minneapolis,
so when they finally got to Oregon,
they were out of bread.
Flat broke, they thought of sleeping
in the car by an open field.

But she remembered grabbing an old
pocketbook from the downstairs hall closet.
Rummaging through her valise, found it,
and inside sparkled a treasure—
together, head to head,
they counted out seven hundred pennies.
He went into the motel rental office;
came out strutting and smiling, so she knew,
though he confirmed it, saying with the joy
of a kid with cotton candy at Coney Island,
"He took it—didn't even count it."

The next morning they saw
the open "field" they'd parked nearby
was really a partially frozen lake
and so they imagined, discussing what if
they'd stayed there and in a fit of passion,
one of them had bumped the hand brake!
They thanked the Lord for their safe-
keeping and for their special bank
of seven hundred bright & shiny pennies.

Part II

Meditations

BUTTERFLY GARDEN

—A quasi-purloined page from the favorite pastime & diversion notebook of lepidopterist & morphologist Vladimir Nabokov, or a found poem

I

In days gone by, you trod Ithaca trails,
the same year I, too, graduate student,
walked at Six Mile Creek, your happy hunting grounds.
But today, you've long been transmuted.
Now, considering form & structure,
I enter alone, a garden's butterfly world.
I own molecular longings to spot you
in one of your own discoveries,
recalling a commentary about crawling leaf-chewing critters
transforming into flying nectar-sipping beauties.

II

I wend & weave my way along paths
noting the fabric of bodies:
wrought of sculptured velvety wings,
or roughly hewn scalloped *coquille Saint-Jacques.*
I spy the Julia, the Coolie, the Isabella.
Ah! and there! the variegated Malachite—
mottled, veined, speckled green,
semi-precious as its gem namesake,
far-traveled from native Trinidad and Tobago.

III

Under a latticework of sky vine,
near the flowered Dutchman's Pipe,
replica cocoon unopened,
yet unfurled is like the full-winged moth,
so like the drooping flower spread.
Oh! mimic me, says nature imitating nature.
Finally, *Da!* dear Vladimir, you spotted an aberration
of the Green Fritillary, and here's the Gulf Fritillary,
light brown, white markings silhouette & etch
confounding doubly, grouped as flower sepals,
a calyx to camouflage
a chrysalis—then pupa's metamorphosis—
voilà! a butterfly enchantress.

IV

I stand stone still,
a Buck-eye brushes my shoulder.
Now on my hand a genera of blue,
not unlike one of yours,
flits to rest, a respite from flight,
on my hand, uncaressable as air & art.
Beside it, the passionflower attracts mimetically
while from a diverse biosphere,
I drench myself,
mirrored genesis,
in the Spice-bush & the Cracker.

THE DEATH OF AUGUST

Last eventide before Corsican starfall
we watched sunfire slip to its descent
beyond the mountain that is Bonifacio.
It startled us
from some profound beached
sleep, dreamless,
promising a moon,
skinny-faced,
ungenerous in proportion.

The Mistral blows—
her force, relentless—
and we are prisoners
incarcerated in this Corsican port,
as Fate wills at the end of August.
Each day we swim
beneath overhanging cliffs
in age-old weather-worn grottoes,
and dig for dinner clams and sea-truffles
with red tongues to garnish spaghetti
cooked in briny water, laced with wine,
consecrated with the finest oil.

Then as stars collide
and unseen meteors collapse,
we sip *pastis*,
sample and savor salmon *paté*;
await the wind's death and tomorrow.
And although a kaleidoscope
of color lies ahead to uplift,
even as leaves fall,
I grieve summer's passing
and the not quite yet demise
of this lingering taste called August.

PIAZZA di SPAGNA

You're on a lunch break, walking in *Piazza di Spagna* near Bernini's
sinking boat fountain, when it hits you among the stop and go

of traffic lights, the *Carabiniere*'s whistles and Charlie Chaplin arm
waves, the bustle of passersby, the honking horns, the sight

of children holding hands, you are alone. And lonely. You yearn
for a past time and, seeing yourself reflected in shop windows,

at once your muscles weary and wilt onto sagging bones. Then
the weight of your years, the heft of your misery gives rise to blanket

your spirit: for wasted moments, for love gone awry, for the anger
in sword-sharp words. The sun peeps through a cloud, a bird

takes flight from a smoky chimney, a wistful guitar melody wends
and wafts its way along concave red tiled rooftops. You hum along

with the old song, *Scrivimi*: an omen to write a letter, and of a sudden
your mood soars with the remembrance of a tiny word spelled: hope

BETWEEN *ITAKA* AND *KEFALONIA*

There's a cutaway reef
between the islands
of Itaka and Kefalonia;
adventurous swimmers
seek it out to dive.

We bask beneath
a cobalt sky
on a smuggler's cliff
then dip into the emerald sea below.

Love sparkles
between us,
as we sail in between islands,
snuggling off island paths
between a host
of pine and olive trees
on the Ionian sea.

At the quay
one late summer morning
in between breakfast and a sail,
lovers wash each other
in an icy communal shower—
cold feet touch
for tiptoe kisses.

Sniffles in stiff
morning air—
a telltale sign
autumn is but a touch away,
distance measured by the wind,
its mourning mantle covers the sky.

A sea of Limbo stretches
between where we're docked
and the sunrise out before us,
indeed, sun and sea blind,
before us, bind with us,
liquid steel in motion,
steaming with the rising sun.
The dying days of August prove
an early fall this year.
I sense the end of summer near;
its finality drawing close.

This first chill—the Mistral's majesty
followed by the rain—all too soon.
Where does the warmth of summer
go chastised between wind and hail?
Where will the summer lovers
now swaddled and sheathed,
quarter over winter?

PHOTO SHOOT

You stand staring at the shore
on jetty rocks strewn in a kidney shape,
colorless paisleys, as if a backstage prop,
as if you'd placed them there one by one.

But how could you lift the Herculean
boulders, standing so silent in the wind,
with your black yoga pants billowing,
and my son's borrowed beige sweater blousing?

I remember buying that knit polo in the Cotswolds
in the heart of England, scattered small towns and villages,
"wool churches," nestled in the hills: stone cottages,
thatched roofs, picture perfect.

That was a year ago. I laughed when you said you loved me,
but now my hands shake as I look into the camera lens, seeing
just how young and lean you are, your face chiseled granite,
and for a time, it's difficult to gauge this shot.

BEACHCOMBER ON HIS BREAK

Your white shirt is open,
the ripples in your abdomen
a reflection of the rippling surf,

water gushes in upon your jeans,
hems let out, not turned up—
you are so much a part

of this natural scene
of weather, ocean, sand
I'd love to paint you as I wait

for you under a golf umbrella
by the lifeguard tower.
Rain drops kiss your face as you roam

bubbly arcs the waves
leave on the compact sand, a healthy break
from a woodworking summer day.

THE BEACH

Your face serious—
a frown mid-brow.
Your lips, corners pulled in,
form a pout;
your eyes scrunch against the sun
to betray the start of crow's feet.
Just above your nose
a line is born of concentration
sometimes meaning lust.

You mean to do a good job;
you mean to go somewhere;
you mean to show someone your intent.
Young. Alive. Reckless.
All movement taut but undulating,
your jeans down below
lean hips, down
to the downy skin beneath
your belly button.

I longed to kiss you there,
once. But now, I'm cold.
Beach water smacks from behind,
rushing up in furrowed waves,
froth, foam, a quick tide, soon
to be drawn back
to the rage of surf.

Why, I ask,
did you never write?
You never called either.
Was it my fault?

That last day—
not even an embrace,
so afraid to touch me,
afraid the combustion
would ignite you
like a roman candle,
or a funeral pyre—
or consume you like a phoenix.
Having subsumed me,
unable to leave me then,
we stood in a sand squall
beneath the arch
of the church loggia
in high dunes.

A pity—for, you see,
I did incinerate
myself for you.
Just think
we could've risen
together … now.
At least high enough
to jump
this next
wave.

MODEL POSING

A picture of you
lying naked
upon a cradle of rocks,
old as Stonehenge,
fetal position
covering your manhood.

The position of your arms
reminds me of *The Thinker*
your closed eyes
in sleepless concentration,
your right breast exposed,
so compressed,
I feel the reverberation,
the beating of your heart
in my own chest.

The vulnerability of your nudity
rekindles the flamed torch
I lofted in air for a year—
my scourge, my flagellation,
my crown of thorns,
and suddenly
the ancient stigmata
of you
comes back to me
bleeding,
pulsating blindly
for a blazing instant

and finally I cry,
the tang of ashes
in my mouth
yet lingers,

but the sores
have scarred over.
The cicatrix of you,
edges of this curled
photograph I took,
are whorls of growth, remembrance …
mere lines on a cockleshell
I trample in the sand.

IN THE CHILL OF A DECEMBER MORNING

Leave love,
a pauper's laundry hanging on trees,
the haze of a winter dawn,
remnant scraps of fog
reminiscent of old curtains,
sheer, sheared, and freezing on the clothesline.

Leave me now with thoughts of how I caressed
your back and stroked your temples
in the garden's gazebo covered with snow,
where the leafless branches of trees
tinkled ice lace to its own melody,

Leave love squeezed tight, wrung out,
used up, finished and diminished,
wind-whipped palio banners in tatters,
pageant proof the race was run.

INTRICACIES OF CICADA WINGS

Today I found cicada wings on the porch.
In the fading light, they look crystallized,

"pearlized" like the insides of an oyster shell
where a grain of covered sand develops into a pearl.

Each segment of the wing is a stained glass window,
the separations like "lead came" or "copper foil"

used in Tiffany lamps and the Rose Window,
high in the south transept of York Minster.

Each division, so precise. Where is the body now?
Gone to its final resting place in the eco-system to nourish

the earth that feeds the tree that the cicada used to feast on.
Herbalists use cicada shells in Chinese medicine;

inhabitants of China eat this insect, and others dine
on it in far off Burma, Malaysia, and the Congo.

I gaze at the transparent, iridescent and shimmering wings
and I am winged away to ancient Greece, where as a handmaiden

to Aristotle we dine on these delicacies. Later, he scribbles a memo
for his *Historia Animalium,* and says to me: Study the cicada,

ancient polyvalent symbol; note in its lifecycle these premises reverberate:
resurrection, immortality, spiritual consciousness and ecstasy.

AMORPHOUS LOVE
— *After JJ Colagrande*

While reading Chekhov
at break-time on the beach,

a discussion looms
like burgeoning clouds filled

with collected rainwater
about to be let loose in a furious storm.

We saunter to the Tiki hut
and sip Long Island tea at the bar.

What is love?
A force that looms large above us?

If you're lovesick, is there a cure? Or is it pure-
ly mental? Can you reason with love?

Love's natural colors range free,
become camouflaged like sand

& dune's defensive scarabs,
or obdurate obsessive reds, the go-getter descending sun.

Some wax cold in morning light's brief fling of bestial blue.
Love's intensity: cymbals crashing in increments

of deafening decibels,
like smelting iron ore

heating from moment
of cool acquaintance

to belt-notched conquest,
fields fallowed, trampled by herds of invading hordes,

concrete poetry limning head-horseman ravishment.
Yet Love drops down dewy from Elysium,

flings into the rapturous ardor of submission—
an atomic heart-shaped arrow

        shewwws from Cupid's bow to pierce.

    BOOM   goes existence!

      Caveat emptor!

"Cupid and my Campaspe played at cards for kisses … Cupid paid."
Love is born on a smeared oily palette, then brushed with spirit
onto a larger-than-life still-life canvas: Frida, Vincent, Claude—

and it consumes. The conflagration everything for a time,
till the pyre's ashes blow into the Ganges.

Love, through ages, likened to a rosebud,
yet its ugly guise,

oh how the thorns rake sharp,
tear & ruddle.

Thorn, thorn,
oh, prickly thorn,

I prick *mi*-self, trickle *mi* prick-
ly bloody wound.

Love, a rose in bloom, textured, layered,
layers, layers of layered complications:

original sin, fragranced by beauty—celebrate it,
celebrate it—celibate it?

Control love? Define love? Mold it? Shape it?
Appreciate & understand it?

Transcendental Love.
Love transmuted, transformed, wilted, dried—

withered potpourri in a ginger jar.
The rain has stopped.

Love is not a thing to josh about;
neither is tossing back

four drinks in an hour,
or the fact I can't love you anymore.

PRIEST

Sunday Mass. I'm late again.
I sit behind the tonsured priest
in alb and amice, a side glance to note
his beatific look a few rows in front of me.
His thoughts cloud above his head,
an aura, a corona, the halo,
he knows he'll garner surely
upon his earthly demise.

Words rise above him.
I look for the comic dialogue's balloon
issuing forth from the mouth.
There is none.
But I can read the words—
in Spanish,
the language of God, the language
of this priest's birth.

He peers ahead at the raised host,
his shoulders lean and edge forward
toward the altar.
His gaze intent, his aesthetic posture
inclines of its own will.
The organ player's notes hang in the air
surrounding priest and thoughts and words.
It's a song I know by rote,

but can't recall the title of, or perhaps
never bothered to learn.
This priest is Spanish.
Not Spanish-speaking
from South America
or Latin-American.

He was born in Spain.
This insistence of Spain

preys upon me because I've been to Avila,
because I know the story of Teresa,
because I've read that she and Juan de la Cruz,
both mystical saints, are two
of the thirty-three Doctors of the Church.
The priest's thoughts of love
of God are in Spanish,
like his deliverance …
though now are pierced with other thoughts
of his aged mother, a widow,
who raised children in a poor
seacoast village in close proximity to La Coruña.
He envisions her cooking *bacalao* and *pulpo;*
inhales sharply and the intake of his breath
takes him by surprise.
He breathes again deeply,

and despite the church incense,
pungent odors of Sunday supper assail him
rich with the perfume of fried garlic
and fish sizzling in hot olive oil,
and once again he tastes *vino tinto,*
as the Holy Chalice is raised.
He strikes his breast three times,
Mea culpa, mea culpa,

mea maxima culpa—
how could I, he thinks,
have lost my concentration,
become distracted
with earthly cares?
And his eyes and my heart
brim with tears
for our salvation.

SUNDAY IN NEW YORK

Some people ride the bus the length
of Manhattan's 5th Avenue, taking in the sights.

They know what it means
when lightening shrieks across a dry sky—

I saw it once in periphery,
but all I could take in was the man

with tastes the same as mine.
Ah, at least I thought they were—

but youth, they say, is blind.
I figured I'd hook that guy

with savory stories of friends & family,
but in truth, he hooked me.

I like my Sundays wet & wild—
drunk on wine & family ties—

I love to cook like *Nonna* did,
a kitchen filled with pungent

aromas: tomatoes boiling down
into a thick red broth for pasta—

that Brooklynites call gravy—
fried zucchini to spread on top.

But oh how I suffered for love
of that bus-rider in the city,

the one with the portfolio
pictures oozing with pride and hope.

Oh, how I ached for love of kin—
Though he'd have kept me

a clichéd wife— summer pregnant,
winter barefoot. But I re-learned myself,

gazing in a mirror, questioning,
dozens of times a day.

There I am! Naked, still young,
wounded & abused,

forlorn but feisty, reciting
prayers for love still with desire!

Shit or shite, as me Irish
bastard bus-rider said.

Here I stand, cooking Sunday dinner
for the kids, humming by a pot

of lamb and Guinness stew,
& at the table, telling Blarney tales,

of his return, wondering all the while,
was I wrong to kick him off my bus?

CRUCIBLE OF YEARNING

I empty my thoughts into a crucible,
the yearning hot; it travels back to images
of squatting figures: fishmongers, roasting meals
on coals off the stern of river barges,
where little ones do wash, mini-adults,
never knowing childhood joys.

Into a carafe, I decant the ache
to hear the snap & slap
of flags in bay breezes
and heed the ring of bicycle bells
that navigate makeshift wharves,
the ting and ping of rain
on the metal siding of garbage scows.

On the quay, women in quilted jackets
and sedge hats carry and transport,
balancing pole and baskets on skinny shoulders.
I regard rickshaw men
hurling curses, through toothless grins
at foreigners, as if their greeting
hailed: Good day.

The specters of my thoughts
cohabitate for such a little while, then
like the cries of hawkers,
dissipate into fog phantoms
carried seaward with the wind.
My thoughts are panderers,
pimps and ponces to the depths of me
wanting total recall.

I crush and pulverize the cuttlebone
and with the white powder
polish all the vessels of sorrow; loss and longing—
they vanish like ghosts shifting in mists
hovering over Aberdeen
and in the flimsy sails of sampans
gliding past fish-laden junks.

EARTH ANGEL
—For Galway Kinnell

This angel who meditates between us
underneath the fibers of our muscles
travels the windless hours of the morn—
a Muse, a Circe, an Egeria.

This angel who meditates between us
metronomes each false heartbeat
between branches blooming with blood oranges
outside the window, nudging every one to birth.

This angel who meditates between us,
witness to a union of souls and minds,
realmed and niched near Earth,
thief-shadow lunging in the breeze.

ALONE AIN'T SO BAD: JOURNAL ENTRY 13,729

I had set the clocks to "Spring ahead." It was just past dawn and since I couldn't sleep anymore, I walked my shepherd on one of the most splendid mornings, alive and tingling with greening all around. We were heading to Shore Road. I am Bay Ridge, is my thought. We strolled the pedestrian pathway near the water from Owls Head Park, imagining what it was like to live in one of the mansions a hundred years ago. Squirrels scampered, jumping from limb to limb in the horse chestnut trees, leaves damp with morning dew. The dog and I turned and I came upon a garbage can on 82nd Street between Ridge Blvd. and Colonial Road. The dog peed on a tree trunk nearby and then sat while I riffled though the can, which was filled to the brim with papers and texts. Most of the books had Ex Libris glued inside beside the name John Paul Jones. They had nautical designs of knotted ropes like *The Ashley Book of Knots* and with anchors too, but wait a sec—wasn't he a very real Navy hero long dead? And wasn't he Scottish? A relative perhaps then is this other JPJ. After looking through all these Navy books and logs, I chanced to see a battered sepia leather journal, whose covers were so faded and scraped that the beige innards of the leather showed at the corners. There was a lock, but no key. I jiggled the closure, and said, "Open Sesame!" and like magic, it sprung open. I rather expected a genie to pop out for the journal begged to be set free from the pile of rubble. I couldn't resist, so I opened to the middle. Here's what was written inside.

Today I called my friend Rita. Three times. She says I really should learn not to obsess, be possessive, or confess all I do to him. He's a bastard. He left me. Rita says I'll get used to it. He said he was going on a photo shoot in Africa—meanwhile he called me from Rome to ask me to save something he forgot to cut out from the Sunday *New York Times* Sports Section. An ad for photos of Native Americans at the turn of the century—not this one, the last one. I'd been home a short while from a conference in the Rockies when he invented this new trip. He also forgot his camera.

Rita's almost 80 and is fine all alone with her books and dog and computer and TV music channel always on, and so I guess am I. This evening my son called to tell me about his stroll in the park with his hunter dog, and how they took a row boat out but the dog hasn't realized yet he's brave or knows how to swim. He fell into the lake. My son jumped in right after him. My son can't swim either. A Marine home on leave, getting a blow job in the next boat, saved them both.

And then I cut the gardenias for a scalloped crystal bowl. The one Gertrude and Louis Miller gave me before they died so tragically, and before they learned that their grandson Andrew was not going to become a doctor, that the little fuck-up knew he was inheriting their fortune, so he left his part-time magazine salesmen's job in Poland and the university dorm where he smoked and sold weed.

The gardenias have never bloomed twice in one year but they did this year, the last year that I'll be in this house by the Narrows. Rita says it's a miracle. I believe in miracles, so I make an aspiration, a wish so intense that the Holy Spirit or some Divinity (in an Elysium I can only imagine) will answer me—surely. Oh, oh the supplication? The same one I always implore to the Heavens above—to have a measure of success before I die. A grand measure, and that he'll come back to me—penitent, contrite, and so, so damn sweet with a hangdog expression in his bag-sad eyes that say: I've been naughty; then he'll want to frolic like a puppy and roll around in the high grass at the top of the knoll. And fuck, fuck, fuck.

I opened one of his "good" wines reserved for the best company—or none at all—so selfish he reserves the right to say when we de-cork one! *Far Niente.* It means nothing—the name of the wine, I mean.

I made a sauce for pasta, spooning in fresh cherry tomatoes like plump grapes into simmering oil with flecks of browning garlic and a smattering of onions, which perfumed the whole kitchen. I tossed in fresh basil that hints of gardenia, and then I pour in the linguini, amalgamated it all with a hit, a dash, a sprinkled fistful of grated *Parmgiano Reggiano.* He loves me because I feed him so well. And so there you have it—a night alone. A last supper Thursday night alone—ain't so very hard to take, knowing he'll come back to me on Friday.

DA PIPERNO

renowned restaurant for artichokes, hugged and nestled in the embrace
of Rome's Jewish Quarter—not far from the Synagogue and my favorite
Bernini fountain where lank, scrawny nude boys reach up to turtle catch.
The sculptor added turtles later, his inspiration gladdens hearts

every time, even depicted in Saro De Domenico's last painting,
before he died, which my pocket, pouch and purse couldn't ransom
from La Galleria "Il Saggiatore" on Via Margutta.
Piperno's, where every sense is heightened; where we dine beneath

square umbrellas, celebrating Carla and Oscar's June anniversary.
We *cin-cin* with Prosecco at Piperno's up a tiny hill from Palazzo Cenci,
steeped with historical deeds and mystery. Thursday nights *bella* Roma
consecrates the rite of fried *baccalá,* and *pasta coi ceci* drizzled green-gold

olive oil on top. In season: *fiori di zucca,* but always *carciofi alla giudia,*
artichokes, yearlong prepared scrumptious Jewish style Da Piperno.
The springtime meal crowned by dessert: *frutta di bosco* (bosk fruits—
wild berries) drenched in cream, or *le palline del nonno,* grandpa's balls,

plump, warm ricotta rounds, dotted with bits of chocolate to enrichen—
wealthy enough to feel one's liver attack the right portion of the body,
devouring them anyway, hoping a walk to nearby Piazza Mattei
to see *la fontana delle tartarughe* will calm the erratic inner organ.

Before the *passeggiata* ending at the fountain, we halt to contemplate
Cenci Palace and Beatrice's brutal patricide—how could she slay
her father? Alberto Moravia's play for posterity so worthy of an hour's
sitting. And once more we leave Piperno's, five senses satiated, plus one.

AUTUMN WALK IN MIZZLING RAIN

At the lake when I walk my dog
round the perimeter, he speaks softly
of things long-ago forgotten.
He's older now and enjoys these serene
moments of remembrance—just he and I again.
The kids grown and me over my empty-nest flutters.
No need to bark and bolt, jolting at the sound of birds
careering in air, chirping, swooping, zooming for the fish.
He reminds me of his swagger days, dash and polished
times, when he'd hidden my slipper for attention,
or the time the police came at 2 AM
because he'd cornered a baby opossum in the fichus.

We move slowly for this fall promenade,
arthritis in his joints and my new knees
a trial getting used to. Leaves eddy and furl
and he scoots to where he thinks a mouse has scurried.
He lifts his head and tells me of the scents
he senses, tiny moles taking up their postings
for the tinge of cold soon to bring white flurries,
and the shoring, storing up of beaver in a stream,
a spring or slough back in the woods.

We round the outer edges of the lake where
someone's prints have smudged in deep
along with a trusty pilot dog that led him home.
It's time for us to go now, sport, what do you say?
He shakes his tail, thrusts his weight on two front paws,
his behind in a dare race me stance.
Not even if I could skip, my friend.

I sit on the wrought iron bench
with wooden back slats
and my patient pal, asks, So what now?

He plops down, resting his head on my feet,
Do you remember, he whispers, as wind
blows my hair and his ears flop a bit,
I do not answer, but lean to stroke his once strong back,
as he whimpers a little
in quick profound old man's sleep,
dreaming of our youth.

PHAN·TAS·MA·GO·RI·A (făn-tăz'mə-gôr'ē-ə, -gōr'-) *n.*

... from the Phantom of the Opera to pheasant under glass, or the roasting
pig stuffed with pine nuts and rosemary in Porta Portesi on hot summer
nights of *ferragosto* when the agora filled to overflowing as on-lookers from
their *pallazzi* with mattresses sticking out from balconies and terraces gazed,
to the tantalizing *pantera* in the park, and under the plane and dogwood
trees in my parent's home on Long Island, the summer that the gazebo was
torn asunder and pushed down in hurricane force winds I knew nothing
about, but certainly would begin to contemplate when I moved to Florida.
Whew, a run-on, or a homerun, a run in a stocking, a runaway, a fugitive,
a stowaway, an escapee, in absenteeism, an absconder, of words, perhaps,
such as a wordsmith, a smithy, a blacksmith, a goldsmith, a changer of
dross into gold, yes, by Giove! an alchemist, who uses an alembic, *alambic,
al-'anbīq ambix, alembicus,* a vial, a vessel, a distiller, a cup that runneth
over, a test tube, a baby, a clone, a fetus, an abortion, the sucker outer,
a vacuumer, a stealer of life, a killer, a murderer, a wonton abandoned
soul, a soulless guileless, giddy gunsmith, and back again to the smithies, a
smithery, a forge, a forger, false, fakery, counterfeit, copy of the old ghost
story of the masked man who loved and lived in the opera house, such as
this phantasmagory prose poem a sort of fantastic sequence of haphazardly
associative imagery, as seen in dreams or the fever that held me in its baker's
arms, warm from the oven, for days when I was an infant and ran with Jesus
in and out of courtyards and arches, then taken by a woman in a brick red
raiment with a hood, and hidden in a tall, woven rush basket with a cover
like an upside down cymbal when the soldiers wearing sandals and thongs,
tunics and breastplates, searched for us to bring us to Herod the Great
during the massacre, but the scene keeps changing, a scene composed of
numerous elements, associations like pure alchemy in the writer's brain, a
definition described in the dictionary online or off, such as this fantastic
imagery, my art.

ROADS

to new beginnings
taper and diverge
to triangulation
and we slide into death

at the hour of Lauds, I meditate
tell me why
we use mud bricks
for a heavy load
or spit into the bottomless pit
of a marble quarry

fighting the wind
we hurl ourselves
into embraces,
blindness thrusts
us to our fate
beneath zodiacs formed by stars
incandescent recollections

while dusk descends
farm hands hoe,
landowners stow tools,
light is consumed
and the last of heaven set afire
by a ginger orb
remembering the Arab prince
unfurling his blue silk prayer rug
as you showed his wife diamonds
rolled like ice upon the velvet gray
plateau, the color of Roman winter sky

I worried so, pregnant, ill,
holed up in a winter shepherd's shed,

baita of succoring warmth
a living desert by the hearth
dry parched prairie earth
balanced on the world's edge
of your knitted blanket
a far cry from the horizon

sun rising, a line of brush burned
by our stable, gusts strong enough to shove
night of the middle universe
cracked open, spewing forth
a fertilized egg
Mars, its progenitor,
or some other planet in between
where starbright souls
gaze at us from unseen eyes

I release myself to wandering
terra firma, Ligurian *Cinque Terre*
placenta of the *al di là*
from nothingness
flecks, sparks, lightning
cleave blackness
falling star fishtails
firebrand moment
the surprised infant
cries at its birthing
horn-of-plenty
splay and spray.

MEDITATIONS

1.

The Hour of Lauds
dawn & *Matins* ...
offer deeds & thoughts
of this unfurling day
rejoice in prayer, the *Angelus;*
in each Sacred Sacramental Canon Hour
remember sick brethren, the dying.
Let the Lord's light shine upon them
for even the desert of the dead trembles
into life as the voice of the Lord
whirls among branches of olive trees,
flaying seedlings.

2.

The Hour of Prime
early morning,
second canonical hour,
the cock crows, three bells fracture
silent autumnal air.
Cum ter reboo, pie Christiferam ter aveto
When I ring thrice, thrice devoutly greet the Mother of Christ.
I take recourse in thee, O Virgin of Virgins, my mother,
recite this *Memorare*
for unwed mothers, mothers birthing, the childless,
abandoned babes, abortionists,
the unborn.

3.

The Hour of Tierce
high morning,
the clock strikes nine
celebration of the Mass
Epiclesis, Holy Spirit,
transform bread & wine into Body & Blood,
later: to hoe, to rake, to dig, to scrape, to plant.
Bless my meditation of Third World Citizens,
traveling tundra, plain, prairie, savannah, foothill;
crossing the Hindu Kush, the Taurus, the Zagros Mountains,
the Syrian Desert & countries of its abode;
Hear! Most Sacred Heart, the laments of the deprived.

4.

Sext
noonday
the refectory:
garden gifts perfume the hall
concentrate, let not hunger permit distraction
Kyrie eleison
beg the guardian enfold me in his wings
bolt the door to the world
Bless us, Oh Lord.
Agnus Dei,
Holy Lamb & Shepherd, forgive our sins,
be mindful of the temporal needs
of the hungry, the poor, the homeless,
the weaknesses of gluttons, debauchers,
the rich, so poor in spirit.

5.

Nones
3 o'clock shadows
begin to canopy
Gloria
reflect, withdraw
My soul doth glorify ...
serene, pastoral reflection
heat, light, sound,
echoes mirroring in pools
in the eyes of my brothers
in puddles along packed-earth pathways—
Ave Maria.

6.

Evensong
sacrosanct
sunset hour of the bells
beckons to the Mystical Body
a call to Vespers
to invoke the Divine Office.
Confiteor
through unfathomable faith,
I confess,
for those unable. I beg forgiveness,
remission, redemption, retribution.

7.

The Hour of Compline
a voice
chimes inside my head:
repose.
Body spent, toil completed.
From the open garret window
a breeze kisses my brow,
Salve, Regina,
Lady of Grace, bearer of goodwill,
instill love in the hearts of men
through the intercession of your son.
Salve, Rex,
restore peace in the world
to souls, to minds, to hearts—
consummatum est
I retire in the arms of the Lord,
my head cushioned
in the lap of my Holy Mother.

PINING

The tree has gone to mulch
carried away unceremoniously out the front door,
down the powdery steps snow-dusted to the arching

curve of our upgrade driveway, hauled off
in the new truck. I've swept the house so very clean
of all the needles of her lovely branches

though the essence of her remains with me
in pine scent, and even sweeping
twelve times twelve, I find fine needles

in the crevices of wooden columns,
in the grout of slates in the mud room,
in the dust goblins I collect with mop or broom.

I loved that tree; I told her what a beauty she was
every day for a month, as I watered her fresh cut stump
in a blue bucket, filling it to the rimless brim.

Such a mother, I worried because
she hadn't supped since the last cup of sugar water
I gave her on that first snowy day we picked her out.

Once a stand-out, stand-alone lonely lovely in a valley field
but while in my house, lacked the company of snow birds,
those nosey magpies from the Wasatch range, or deer who'd butt

and scratch their heads against her, the morose moose left nearby
in a hollow—alone she rendered us a living-room full
of mirth and joy and light and love and beauty

with reminiscences in countless decorations,
she wore with panache for such a simply dressed girl.
I begged her forgiveness as I fed her glucose

and gallons of water each day for the ultimate sacrifice
of giving up her young, muscular body, her simple forest life.
She was ten feet tall—never had a tree so lofty,

skirted with a fullness like crinoline slips—
never had one so shapely, exuding health still
till this very day from ultra pungent waxy needles

short, strong, thick arm branches that held lacy angels—
why if she'd been a guy, you'd imagine a stevedore's forearms,
bulging, hands suntanned, huge and gnarled

from work at the Brooklyn Navy Yard,
gone home now to cradle in those two hands,
with incredible tenderness, a pale, naked infant.

LEAVES & GLASS

From the pool cabana to the etched glass encased porch,
she strides among leaves that swirl in a feverish frenzy—

along with madding hummingbirds—puzzle pieces hurled
willy-nilly, insistent as the smell of apples ripening

in a basket on the wrought iron table. Glancing out from the wavy glass
room, waiting—a keen observer of curled and desiccated leaves

from centennial yard trees being swept away like dreams. Everything's
afire—all aglow now are the coals in the brazier, the leaves ochre and red,

like Rome's soccer team, colored pineapple golden and strawberried,
a perennial mix like yellow-edged burgundy roses,

equipped with thorns, withering in the porcelain blue vase.
These falling leaves eddy and churn, hit porch windows and roof

like birds diving, mimicking spring with dizzying madness.
There's joy in these flight patterns, song in wind gusts,

electricity in pre-storm air that ignites flames to warm heart and hearth.
Yet, she, lone sparrow, misses him enough to cry out,

"When will I fly free from this tree of life to meet you whirling
in limitless sky, boundless space, my spirit flitting along with yours?"

LA BODEGA

You in a sombrero, wide leg
gaucho pants and a cape—
you could be Zorro.

I witness your tango,
crafted of intricate steps—
climbing sky-scraper promises,
calves intertwined, separating,
cascading outward spins—
dancers slither, slide,
stretch to link
a commingling
nouveau flurry pattern.

Your steps, a flinging recklessness,
wanton in abandon—stab reticent & taciturn,
a stiletto flash in the dimlit dancehall.
The artistes stumble and stagger,
strident bidders of brash romance
& the tyranny of ardour, worshipful of hope;
if one halts, hesitates, or falls,
one partner remains still,
still proffering a hand
to stand & stabilize.

The chiaroscuro club,
La Bodega,
witnesses the final thrusts
& swirls
with dizzying swoosh
of silktight thighs
whipped to froth by a frenzy
of satin skirt,
a crescendo tailspin,

riotous with cymbal crash,
exalting the devastating
end of the sinking
bowery
of despair—
this ballet,
your dance,
my love.

YOUR NAME

As sunrise, thin and tenacious
Yearns toward summer,
Fragile shadows scrub away darkness.
Your lust, diamond of love,
Succumbs to dreams
And sleep that evade me.

At my desk a lamplight sheds
A bright circle on a manuscript left open
At a page I've orchestrated poorly.
I sew a white button on your blue shirt,
Then set it aside to write your name in bold block letters
With blood from a finger pricked by the needle.

I tear the piece of paper,
Scrunch it into a tiny ball,
And as light of day streaks across your face,
And dust motes groan and glide away
Into a stream of pure light,
I close my eyes in sleeplessness.

In the morning sun of a Jerusalem day,
I mount a folding chair by the Wailing Wall.
On tiptoes, I stretch my arm high above my veiled head
And squeeze the paper into a crevice
Where even now my prayer for you abides
Till it and we are dust.

TRAVELLING

in the gait of a fox
in need of rest,

I couch myself
upon a feather
bed of ease.

But then I feel
the earth open
beneath me
and a spectral hand

reaches up to touch me,
and the grasp
carries away the baby
nestled so snugly,
so wanted in my womb.

THYME, TIME & THINGS GREEN

Thyme and sage and basil's feathery
Tops round the birdbath
Short shorts in Point Lookout
Hotels and properties in Monopoly
Shamrock keychain on bike handlebars
Cat's eye marbles and a dead frog
Plume moss on a shady knoll
Jack in the Beanstalk.

Ecclesiastical Ordinary Time
Pews decorated with green sateen
And white ribbons on Communion Day
Birthday corsage with olive grosgrain bows
St. Patrick's Day and green plaid uniforms
Blooming magnolia trees on Colonial Road
Lily of the valley's pointy leaves in purple pansy beds
Tumbling and rolling down a grassy slope.

Grandma's kitchen at dusk, sprigs of mint for tea
"Parsley, sage, rosemary and thyme: Will you be of Wicca, tonight?"
Zucchini, spinach, the lettuce-faced clock
Clover, cress and celery
Lawn and ferns and feathered badminton cocks
Nettle and ivy
The bus home.

The drapes of Tara for Scarlett's dress
Lush velvet trim on my ruffled gown
Holly nosegay: stephanotis and baby's breath
Christmas wrapping
Malachite earrings
An emerald class ring
A jade bracelet
The verdant insistence in his eyes.

The lettering on Eco writer #2 pencils
Neon nights in Harlem
Wreath & Foil sorority blazer
Bikini panties
His convertible
The stamp on his farewell letter
At summer's end; enclosed within
Crisp hundred dollar bills in a Stone Bank envelope.

The stoplight at the corner of the clinic
An open-backed nightshift
Doctors' scrubs and wet prep soap sponges
Glowering halogen lights on the walls
The operating table
The sea greenness of the nurse's shadow
Bridesmaid dresses, seed pearls on loose threads
Fall to the floor like tears.

SANDALS

The night begins at dusk.
Esperanza, hope, life's breath itself,
slips narrow feet
into high-heeled sandals,
sexy "*putana* shoes,"
stiletto spikes an invitation—
a "come hither" beckoning.

On the street,
he drives past slowly,
sliding down a glacis to a stop sign
canopied by summer plane trees
on the road to *Rubra Saxa*.

A stunner struts past his car—
an insouciant walk in sandals
shining beneath the streetlight.
The footwear, phosphorescent of silver gilded straps,
an open-toed beauty, designed of strips of isinglass
lime green leather so hot that in the streetlamp it pinks,
Marilyn Monroe molded in a magenta sheath,
with cross-cuts clasped by a broche crimson of rubies
and Russian amber crown jewels
at the toes he knows are lacquered.

Crouched behind the wheel he cranes his neck.
His lank view spies a sculptured ankle,
supple legs, knees that know how to kneel,
tan thighs below a white mini skirt—
an invitation to lust in a synthetic love tryst,
a romp, a trundling of moist parts on a strange bed.

He honks the horn.
Leaning on the street lamp,
she turns, smiles, and waves,
but as this *travestito* approaches the car,
the driver speeds away,
not yet ready for new games to begin.

PINK SATIN BALLET SLIPPERS

hung for years in back of my closet,
appended like the bouquet of dried yellow roses
from the left corner of my dresser mirror.
When did I discard the shoes, the flowers,

the dancing dreams & ballerina hopes?
Today's mail tossed upon
the polished mahogany table—
an invitation from Northern Trust.

Inside the creamy envelope
a shiny card, a photo in shadowy
powdery light: pink satiny
ballet slippers crisscrossed

among yellow rose petals
so real, so beautiful,
they perfume the entranceway.
Opening the card, a cordial

invitation with *R. S. V. P.*
The Miami City Ballet Company's
performance—a recital with my own name,
this love and betrayal ballet—*Giselle.*

BELSITO SUNDAY MORNING

Through the arcade I see him.
He crouches low over *il braciere.*
The scent of roasting chestnuts
reaches out to warm me.
Gray-ghost, after-Mass mist dissipates,
seeing his smile of greeting.
The stubble-bearded aging face gives way
to youthful eyes as shoulders straighten.
And though I have no desire for his respite,
I always buy a thousand *lire* worth
just to see the gnarled hands shuffle once more
plump brown nuts in his selection.
"Only those well done," his voice assures,
and wraps them in a cone of paper
from *Gente* or *Oggi*—
as precious as wild violets unearthed
among asparagus in Spring.
Then that old face flashes its toothless smile.
He says the wind is *tramontana.*
I nod my head.
Black fingers wave as I turn to go.
I cross the street, steal a backward glance,
see his shoulders hunch to brace tomorrow's wind.

I DREAM YOUR VOICE

In dreams, your voice comes to me.
In sleep, I hear hypnotic rhythms.

Your voice raises me up, pitches me toward you,
I follow its strains for I am at once

somnambulist and slave. I kneel before you,
I kiss you, but you do not stir or speak.

Your voice, a memory so profound,
follows me back to bed, follows me into sleep,

inconstant as patches of warm water
in a bath, mesmerizing ebb and flow

like the soft sound of water rushing
the pilings of a dark wharf.

Again I am facing you and I kiss you,
but as before you do not rouse or talk.

Your voice, nothing but a sweet recall,
shadows me to cushioned sleep, to dream

its soothing draw and gush, the moving sound
of water's plash against the deep dock struts.

LIMERICK

Not far from the Jurys Hotel in Limerick over the bridge spanning cold,
dark, swift-running Shannon riverwater, a sweater shop ensconced

invitingly bids us welcome. He selects and buys me a cotton pullover,
color of South Florida January sky when sun teetering on the brink

ventures into Aquarius. Appliquéd, stitched, embroidered seahorses,
starfish, cockleshells almost heart-shaped rounds puff out, wrinkled,

puckered, rough to touch, striated ribs radiating to scalloped closure
tempting enough to slit open and eat salty raw from the sea like I did

as a child summering in Point Lookout. There, I crossed barefooted
over open stretches out back of the cottage—oasis flatland of broken

shells till my feet gained purchase on flat jetty rocks where Grandpa
fished for fluke and flounder; where I, skinny-belink, hell-bent

without wheels, yanked mussels, beards clumped lava-black, deep
beneath the water playground for red starfish, redder beyond reach

as I swam kicking spindly legs, slapping unskilled arms, gulping
Atlantic mouthfuls, spewing forth a whale spout spray between

giggles and cries for help. Grandpa fishes me out and with treasure trove
of seafood bagged we march, triumphant soldiers, legions of Caesar

Augustus, returning to Rome from Ostia Lido, straight into the ocean-
fronted kitchen that faced the sea. Mom sautés black ovals, almost orbs,

never once partaking with Grandpa, while I, curious minx, mix
of toughened feet, tanned arms by sun's refracting rays through salt

water, reach a reedy hand, dare to sample and divine, salmon-tinged
meat womb-nestled vulva in shiny mother-of-pearl. My tongue probes

spongy meat, brinally sweet of ocean billows captured cooked flavor,
as delectable as clams dug with feet from bay's muddy clay bottom

only yesterday—bivalves christened cherrystones, shells like cockles.
My fingers turn the pages and I read journal entries and remember

lilting names: Kilarny, Tralee, Ring of Kerry right-hand driving
on the left to Dublin where, in pubs, we ate fish chowders splendid

of tawdry cockles, clams, mussels. I bow a sequined ribbon round
the notebook like praying hands entwined with a corona of rosary

beads, while ejaculations of hope fall from my lips—supplications
for February's genesis, blue-bright skies, crystalline clear,

cold, cold enough to wear an Irish sweater and stroll
the beach in search of cockle shells and myself.

82ⁿᵈ STREET, BROOKLYN
—*For Peter Balakian*

I wish I had a photograph of the blooming magnolia tree
    across the street from my red brick house the day I found
    a box of teacher's gold stars strewn beneath it.

How I want to go back to dodge-ball days
    in front of Carrabba's sprawling white mansion when Billy
    gave me a ride on the handlebars of his black Schwinn bike.

I wish I could trace my initials carved on the trunk
    of the huge horse-chestnut tree, squirrels dartling
    from branch to branch, brown nuts falling on my head.

If I close my eyes I can watch myself scale the garage
    in back of my house, and on its roof, catch guitar music
    wafting toward me on a gentle summer breeze.

Ah! for a slice of childhood: I long for peanut-buttered evenings,
    playing stickball on 82ⁿᵈ Street, hearing my mother call me
    in for dinner under a sprinkling wink of golden stars.

WINTERSCAPE

The skeletal branches of the trees
hold the night's snow,
that in the morning sun
is a raiment of silver and gold.

I waited for you through the storm
with candles lit
brightly in the window
and the hearth aglow.

You didn't come. You called, the staticky line
of the cell phone muffled your words,
like the muffler full of snow
of your stalled car left on the highway.

You had to hoof it to a motel.
I cannot but wonder what she looked like ...
the object of your stalling.
After a solitary breakfast

of oatmeal, blueberries and cream,
sprinkled with brown sugar,
I wonder if her tawny skin shows
crinkly smile lines at the corners of her eyes too.

COTTONWOOD CANYONS
—For William Stafford

Dawn ascends as I crest the summit;
my truck's headlights shine upon a carcass
in the narrow twist of road. I hesitate then stop dead,
grab a flashlight from the glove compartment
and walk along the embankment's edge.

A ten point buck, magnificent in the throes of death,
lays on his side, legs thrashing, lashing, twitching.
A long breathy sigh fills the ghostly air before sunup,
echoing through the gorge, entering my soul for eternity.
I kneel to touch his neck for pulse. He's gone. Eyes fixed.

Last images of near-escape frozen on corneas becalmed—
stilled, forever benign. Words of sorrow issue from my mouth.
Hesitating, I cry out and beg forgiveness for this sin, release a prayer
for redemption's sake. Upon my lips, I taste salty tears and fear
of my own demise, as I roll him off the precipice into the canyon below.

APACHE TEARS

Black obsidian,
weathered nodules,
line the road.

Obsidian with patterns of snow
like star showers,
other designs too,
lay frozen in the snowflake stone.

These volcanic rocks
once blanketed the land,
the way woven blankets
once covered the floors of tepees.

They tell an age-old story,
a sad tale of genocide,
of greed for land,
of dominance.

Here, if you look long enough,
deep enough,
you will see pale face prowess—
splashes of white on a moonless night.

TOLSTOY'S KREUTZER SONATA

What of Pozdnuishef's crime, now that her corset's
Bones are heaped in bloody tatters?

His final sadistic deed in the crystal night,
Spurious proxy, recompenses.

She whimpers as he exhales:
If the train had moved but slower.

His anguished soul, flaked and covered
By snow and remorse, latent homoerotic desires—

A woodland journey swarming
Full of regret and *amour* not for her, but the lover.

The husband covets the last of her tale,
Yet she confesses not, nor does he shrive to absolve.

Quivering above her, he stands, a frozen
Winter landscape, as if to quiet breath

All malady becoming possessed,
A Beelzebub unleashed. The fetid air,

Repulsed by snow's desquamate rapture,
Waxes Siberian like his anger vented

To accost every thought, her mandates
Gone to naught in the remembrance

Of the piano duet. The sonata's music
Executed with panache, like this death

That holds swell in the icy corridors
As he sits with loaded revolver and newspaper,

A veritable icon at his desk—a recital unto himself—
While a dagger dropping to the floor

Is a symphony in blood, near the nursery
Where laughter and joy,

Vexed by misdeeds and conceits
No longer issue forth.

And of the beloved—nothing.
And of her body—nothing.

All upended and ended, the severe beauty
In her glistening, glistering feverish eyes,

Futile *andantino* and rousing
Crescendo in a concert stilled.

MY ABSENT HUSBAND
—For Peter Balakian

For the rainfall's ripples on the silvery, slate water of the Tiber
For the walks on the cobblestone streets to Cinema *Pasquino*

Our youth comes hurtling back
Our youth comes hurtling back

For the spaghetti *all'olio* at 2 AM after playing bridge at Club *Amici*
For the clams I cleaned on Capri, dockside of our boat, the *Miadidi*

Our youth comes hurtling back
Our youth comes hurtling back

I throw kisses to the past, wave my hands, watching a handkerchief
embroidered with your initials blow away.

I fling arms full of letters, full of photos, full of *riso amaro*,
bitter rice, tossed on our wedding day 41 years ago.

How could our youth not come careering back?
How could it not come plunging, crashing, colliding back?

STORM IN SAN FELICE CIRCEO
—For Samuel Coleridge

The storm,
not yet arrived this autumn eve, is ushered in with howling wind—
celestial strangers flapping wings that blow the leaves and branches
of the poplars into whips to lash against my window and scourge and flail
the porticoes and loggia of the *palazzo* down the road.
I see it in the distance when lightening cracks the sky—
illumined by ungodly brightness and wonder if the old ones fare well
in the shacks beside the arbor. Do they dream of youth or hardy disposition?

Silence now.
Except for rustling sheets and coverlet, my baby stirring in his cradle.
I approach him, who wanders among elves and angels in the Land of Nod.
I take hold of his chestnut crib, and seeing my hands, I visualize others,
gnarled, misshapen at the joints, whose contorted unloveliness
made this miraculous carved wooden construction of useful purpose.
Here within lies constrained my only child asleep, who, even in the folly
of his dreams, is unable to fall, crashing unrestrained to the tile floor.

I behold
the cheek on which he doesn't rest, so puffed and pink,
kissed by Circean sun these penultimate days of October.
I can't help but touch his hair so fine, his cheek,
a Raffaello's *putto* envies, or at least resents a little.
I stand barefoot and begin to shiver, my toes curl, the way my husband
says they do when I'm uncertain, or when I ask him for the very moon,
when only stars are in his pocket. I've delayed covering my feet,
so fascinated was I by the storm's approach. Now cold and slipperless,
I drape my shoulders with a shawl crocheted before my baby's birth.
I pull on hunting socks thick enough to serve as boots.
Though they are huge, as are my husband's feet, they're warm
as August sunlight on the sand near the old Saracen tower.

The weekend's over;
alone now, except for the little one, and, yes, the company of fear
of storms, remembering how storm-caught at sea along the fjords
of Jugoslavia—was it summer '79? We sailed into a bay and threw
two anchors. One by one my husband took the ropes, dancing snakes
writhing in black water, pulling, yanking them along into his skiff.
Tying ropes together, we fastened portside, the other aft. When he reached
shore, he circled a tree, fastening the ropes, accompanied by our hopes.
I watched him, soaked in draping yellow slicker, hood flapping like a flag
on sunburned shoulders burdened by jacket's weight. Then the calm.
Towards daylight rowdy revelers, drunk and laughing, docked a stone's toss
from a shack we'd glimpsed earlier. By morning they were gone,
or had they never been? We saw great stretches of moon land, dotted
with craters and barren earth on each side of us. While he checked the map,
I snuggled in his powder-blue mohair I'd made when last in London.
The scent of his Cerrutti on the pillow.

I sense
the pitch and roll of that night, dizzying me still. And in any storm, real
or imagined, I feel each nerve ending jump and jolt and wish for fetters
to tie me down. At creaking sounds, my palms begin to sweat.
I hear a knock. A guest at this hour? The barn door unhasped? Or loosed
to further wind beatings? Again the church bells chime the hour in San
Felice's church on *La Cona*. Hoofbeats break against the sodden fields,
the outside quietude shattered by a cantering demon, flying fast across
the land in a black cape, and on the fleet shadow a horse festooned
in funereal plumes. Is this Ichabod Crane? Or a presage of crepe to come?
Some unknown grief, the like of which I jettison from dreams a thousand
times, a thousand times, a thousand times and more while we are parted.

My heart races faster.
knowing my husband-traveler's gone abroad again. The swift-pulsing
of my blood does not permit me sleep—afraid of dangers that shadow him,
there, and me, here. I do not know what torments me or why, but can I cast
all fear into the storm's eye to fend for itself?

This night of specters, waits, weighted with wraiths, viragoes, witches
conjured up by storm. What would I give to banish them as in days of yore
or olden times? Just say, Diminish. Be gone! Foul, unnamed daymares.

I rush
to find a candle as the lamps are out. I stumble toward the window,
overlooking meadow. I see the horseman traced in milky moonglow
and the swift-moving clouds of darkest grey turn to jet.
Is this a memory, a trick? Does this night rider truly gallop with his steed
to sail with wings across a brook in the fallow field outside
our boundaries' garden? That field where only yesterday
I gathered remnant berries, blacker than any summer
yield, a gift left from the birds. In untamed thickets, I gleaned
among strawberry grapes grown wild. The creepers, choked by brambles,
cut and scratched my arms. But even as the vines gasped for breath,
they hosted clinging ivy, entwining glories, whose morning habit
opens them before the stroke of midday sun—a tangle of cups, trumpets,
inverted bells, azure as a summer sky and more.

Now frenzied
bolts crackle in the darkest sky, then cease, abating with the wind. I clutch
my nightgown at the throat, listening to water torrents drench the antique
pump, drown the pail below, flood the stone sink Baptismal font
underneath the apricot arbor. And what of the kittens left cozy warm
in the basket lined with ticking? A hopeful sigh escapes me;
a tiny supplication heavenward for their safekeeping, hoping *mamma gatto*
had feline sense to shelter them somewhere in the barn.

I listen
to sheep bleating in pens while shutters beat away and rattle against the stout
stone walls. Thunderheads drum, deafening my entreaty that this deluge
does not hammer free young apples budding in the orchard.
A tiny sneeze ushers me cribside once more. Is he cold? His arms thrash
the air, eyes open wide in a bright stare, seeking comfort and refuge
in my arms. I raise him to my breast. Ah, babe, I croon, You're safe.

This storm
will soon be chased away, along with all my silly fears—goblins
gone to haunt the cemetery knoll beyond the hill of our boundary fences.
A lie to soothe, for I wonder if the horseman waits below to thwart, to wreck
apocalyptic havoc on this Hallows Eve of the Feast of All Good Saints.

About Nina Romano

NINA ROMANO earned an M.A. from Adelphi University and an
M.F.A. in Creative Writing from Florida International University. She
lived in Rome, Italy, for twenty years where many of her poems and stories
are set.

Her short fiction, memoir, reviews, and poetry have appeared in *The
Rome Daily American, The Chrysalis Reader, Whiskey Island, Gulf Stream
Magazine, Grain, Voices in Italian Americana, Vox, Chiron Review, The
Salt Lake City Weekly, Mangrove Review*, and *Irrepressible Appetites,* among
others.

Excerpts from her novel-in-progress, *The Secret Language of Women*, have
appeared in *Dimsum: Asia's Literary Journal, Southern Women's Review*, and
Driftwood.

Romano's debut poetry collection, *Cooking Lessons*, was published in June
2007 by Rock Press.

CPSIA information can be obtained at www.ICGtesting.com
Printed in the USA
LVOW040358191112

307894LV00001B/21/P